Making the Past into Presents

Jo Brooker

Heinemann is an imprint of Pearson Education Limited,
a company incorporated in England and Wales, having
its registered office at Edinburgh Gate, Harlow, Essex, CM20 2JE.
Registered company number: 872828
www:heinemann.co.uk

Heinemann is a registered trademark of Pearson Education Limited

First published 2000
Original edition © Reed Educational & Professional Publishing Limited 1998
Literacy World Satellites edition © Reed Educational & Professional Publishing Limited 2000
Additional writing for Satellites edition by Wendy Cobb

16
11

ISBN 9780 43511892 1

ISBN 9780 435 11892 1   *LW Satellites: Making the Past into Presents* single copy

ISBN 9780 435 11896 9   *LW Satellites: Making the Past into Presents* 6 copy pack

All rights reserved. No part of this publication (except the templates) may be reproduced or transmitted in any form, or by any means, electronic or mechanical, including photocopy, recording or any information storage and retrieval system without permission in writing from the publishers.

Designed by M2
Printed in Great Britain by Ashford Colour Press Ltd

Acknowledgements

Photos
Telegraph Colour Library, cover and page 10. Ronald Sheridan / Ancient Art and Architecture Collection, pages 8 and 16. Brian Wilson / Ancient Art and Architecture Collection, contents page top, page 4 top and page 12. C M Dixon, pages 5 top, 14 and 18. All other photos by Keith Lillis.

Illustrations
Oxford Illustrators, pages 6 and 7.

Models and art direction by Jo Brooker.

Also available at Stage 1 of *Literacy World Satellites*

ISBN 9780 435 11893 8   *LW Satellites: Incredible Insects* single copy
ISBN 9780 435 11897 6   *LW Satellites: Incredible Insects* 6 copy pack

ISBN 9780 435 11891 4   *LW Satellites: The Search for Tutankhamen* single copy
ISBN 9780 435 11895 2   *LW Satellites: The Search for Tutankhamen* 6 copy pack

ISBN 9780 435 11894 5   *LW Satellites: How a Book is Made* single copy
ISBN 9780 435 11898 3   *LW Satellites: How a Book is Made* 6 copy pack

ISBN 9780 435 11900 3   *LW Satellites: Teacher's Guide Stage 1*
ISBN 9780 435 11899 0   *LW Satellites: Guided Reading Cards Stage 1*

Contents

Introduction 4
Who made the artefacts? 6
Egyptian necklace 8
Egyptian pyramid 10
Greek coins 12
Greek temple photo frame . . 14
Roman scroll 16
Roman draughts board 18
Templates 20
Book list 23
Index 24

Introduction

People have always made things. You can see some of them here. Some are big and some are small. The temple is very big. The coins are very small. They were all made by people who lived long ago.

All these things are called artefacts. Artefacts can help us understand the people who made them.

This book shows you how to copy some of these old artefacts. Follow the step-by-step instructions and you will have some works of art to keep or to give away. Have fun turning the past into presents!

Who made the artefacts?

The Egyptians

People started to live near the River Nile in about 5000 BC. We call these people Ancient Egyptians. They made tools and boats. They also made smaller things like pots and jewellery.

This map of Egypt shows where people lived in 3000 BC. Their homes were in cities along the banks of the River Nile.

The Greeks

People have lived in Greece for thousands of years. From about 2000 BC, they began to build cities. There they built temples to their gods and made many artefacts.

This map shows how the Ancient Greeks settled all round the Mediterranean Sea. By 300 BC all the orange parts of this map belonged to Greece.

The Romans

In 700 BC, Rome was just a little town in Italy. But it grew into a very big city and its army took over other countries. Roman artefacts have been found in all these countries.

The purple parts of the map show where the Romans had settled by 120 AD. The Romans took over much more land than the Greeks.

Egyptians

Greeks

Romans

500 BC   0   AD 500

Egyptian necklace

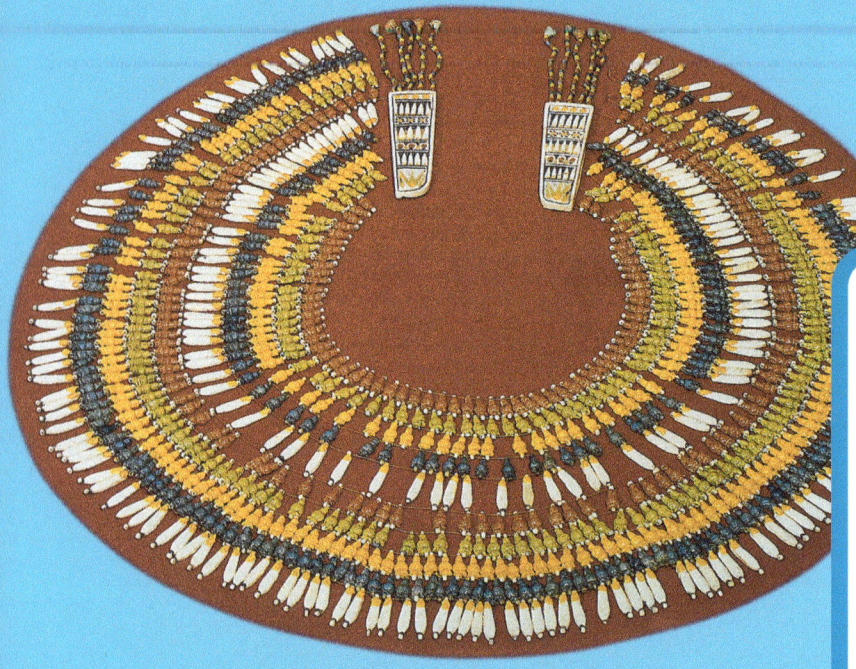

This necklace is made of clay beads. It was found in the tomb of Tutankhamen.

The people of Ancient Egypt loved jewellery. Both men and women wore necklaces, bracelets and anklets.

Materials

* pasta tubes — small packet
* paints
* felt — 34cm long, 26cm wide
* thick card — 12cm long, 6cm wide
* glue
* string — 50cm long
* beads

Equipment

* paintbrush
* white crayon
* hole punch
* scissors

Method

- Paint the pasta tubes in different colours. Let them dry.

- Ask your teacher for a template.

- Place part A of the template on the felt. Use the white crayon to draw round it.

- Cut out the felt shapes.

- Place part B of the template on the card and draw round it.

- Do this again. Then cut out the two shapes.

- Punch out the two holes.

2
- Paint the card shapes and let them dry.
- Look at the photo. Lay out the felt and card shapes as shown.
- Glue the card shapes to the felt.

3
- Work out your pattern. Put the tubes next to each other on the felt. Start in the middle of the small curve.
- When you are happy with your pattern, glue the tubes into place.
- Let them dry.
- Do the same for the other two curves.

4
- Cut the string in half.
- Put a piece of string through each hole.
- You could put more tubes on the strings.
- Tie a knot at the ends of the strings.

Egyptian pyramid

The Ancient Egyptians buried their dead kings and queens in pyramids. The biggest ones took 20 years to build.

These are the great pyramids at Giza, near Cairo.

Method

- Ask your teacher for a template.

- Put the template on the card and draw round it.

- Cut it out.

- Use the pencil and ruler to draw the dotted lines.

- Use the knitting needle to score them.

- Label flap A and side A.

Materials
* card – 30cm long, 18cm wide
* glue
* paint
* big sheet of paper
* glitter or sand

Equipment
* pencil
* scissors
* ruler
* knitting needle
* paintbrush

1

2
- Bend along the lines till you have made a pyramid.
- Glue flap A to side A.

3
- Glue the other 3 flaps to the bottom.
- Paint the pyramid and let it dry.
- Draw some Egyptian pictures on it.
- Put the sheet of paper on the table. Lay the pyramid on one of its sides.
- Use a brush to paint glue over the lines of your picture.
- Tip glitter or sand over the glue.

4
- Shake the pyramid gently over the paper.
- Collect the spare glitter or sand.
- Turn the pyramid so that a new side is on top.
- Do the same to all the sides.

Greek coins

Greek coins were made of gold or silver. Many of them had a picture of a god on one side. The other side had a mark to show where the coin was made.

This coin shows Pegasus, the flying horse.

Materials
* plasticene
* talcum powder
* air hardening clay
* gold or silver paint

Equipment
* rolling pin
* small plastic toy animal
* soft paintbrush

Method

- Roll up a ball of plasticene. Make it the size of a small tomato.
- Roll up a ball of clay the same size.
- Put the ball of clay on one side, to use later.
- Use the rolling pin to make the plasticene ball into a disc.
- Press the toy into the disc. Pull it off very carefully. You now have a mould.

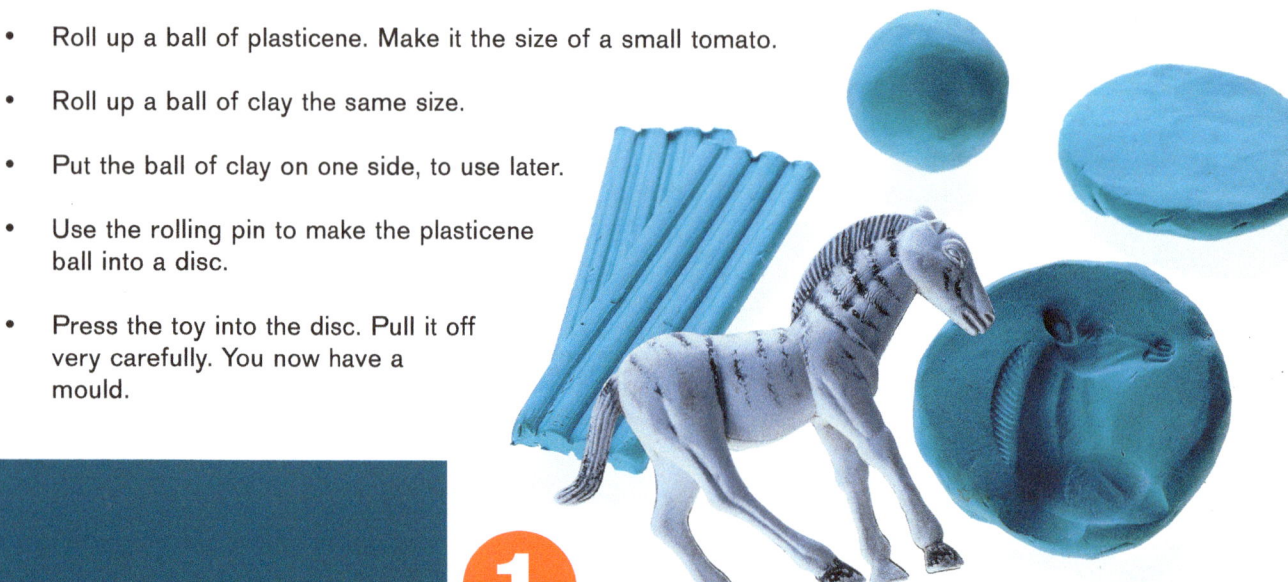

1

- Use the brush to spread powder over the mould.

- Take your ball of clay and flatten it into another disc. This should be a bit smaller than the plasticene.

- Put it on top of the plasticene and press it into the mould.

- Roll over the clay with the rolling pin.

- Pull the plasticene off the clay.

- Make sure the clay is flat.

- Leave the clay to dry.

- When it is dry, paint it gold or silver.

Greek temple photo frame

The temple of the Greek god, Neptune.

The Ancient Greeks had many different gods and built temples for them. They thought the gods lived in these temples when they came to Earth.

Materials
* card – 30cm long, 22cm wide
* corrugated paper – 14cm long, 8cm wide
* sticky tape
* corrugated cardboard – 5cm long, 5cm wide
* glue
* gravel or small stones

Equipment
* pencil
* scissors
* ruler
* knitting needle

Method

- Ask your teacher for a template.

- Put part A on the card and draw round it. Cut it out.

- Use a pencil and ruler to draw the dotted lines.

- Score them with the knitting needle.

- Bend along the lines to make a temple shape.

- Put part B on the corrugated paper and draw round it.

- Do this again. Then cut out the two shapes.

- Make small cuts in each end of the shapes.

- Bend each shape round to make a tube. Tape the joins.

- Fold out the cut ends to make flaps.

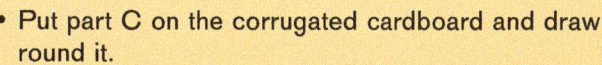

- Put part C on the corrugated cardboard and draw round it.

- Do this again. Then cut out the two shapes.

- Glue the flaps of one tube to one of the squares.

- Do the same with the other one. Let them dry.

- Glue the squares on top of the pillars to each side of the temple.

- Glue the bottom flaps of the pillars to the base of the temple.

- Let them dry.

- Stick stones on the bottom of the temple. Leave a gap at the back for the photo.

- Draw a pattern on the front of the temple.

- Put a photo in from the side.

Roman scroll

The Ancient Romans wrote on scrolls. The scrolls were made of papyrus. Papyrus is made from the stem of a plant. It looks like crinkly paper.

This stone carving shows a teacher reading from a scroll.

Materials
* white or cream sugar paper
* brown paint or cold tea
* bamboo a bit wider than the sugar paper
* glue
* ribbon

Equipment
* big paintbrush
* pencil
* felt tip pen

Method

- Tear the edges of the paper. Make them look ragged.

- Paint the front and back with thin brown paint or cold tea.

- Let it dry.

1

2
- Glue the bamboo along the top of the paper.

3
- Use a pencil to write a poem or a letter on your scroll.
- Go over the pencil lines with a felt-tip pen.

4
- Roll up the scroll.
- Tie it with the ribbon.

Roman draughts board

Here are some Ancient Romans playing a board game.

The Ancient Romans liked playing games. They played ball games and wrestling. They liked board games, too.

Materials

* thick card – 30cm long, 30cm wide
* dark paper – 40cm long, 40cm wide
* glue
* magazines
* air hardening clay
* paint

Equipment

* scissors
* pencil
* paintbrush

Method

The board

- Cover one side of the card with glue.
- Stick the card in the middle of the paper.
- Cut off the corners of the paper.
- Glue the edges of the paper down on to the card.

2

- Ask your teacher for a template.
- Trace or copy it on to the card.
- Choose two colours.
- Find pictures with these colours in the magazines.
- Cut out lots of squares in each colour. These should be a little smaller than the squares on the board.
- Glue the squares on to the board as shown in picture 4.

The counters

- Roll the clay into 24 small balls.
- Flatten them into discs and let them dry.
- Paint 12 of them to match one set of the squares on your board.
- Paint the other 12 discs the other colour.

3

4

Templates

Note to the teacher: each template should be enlarged to 200% on the photocopier.

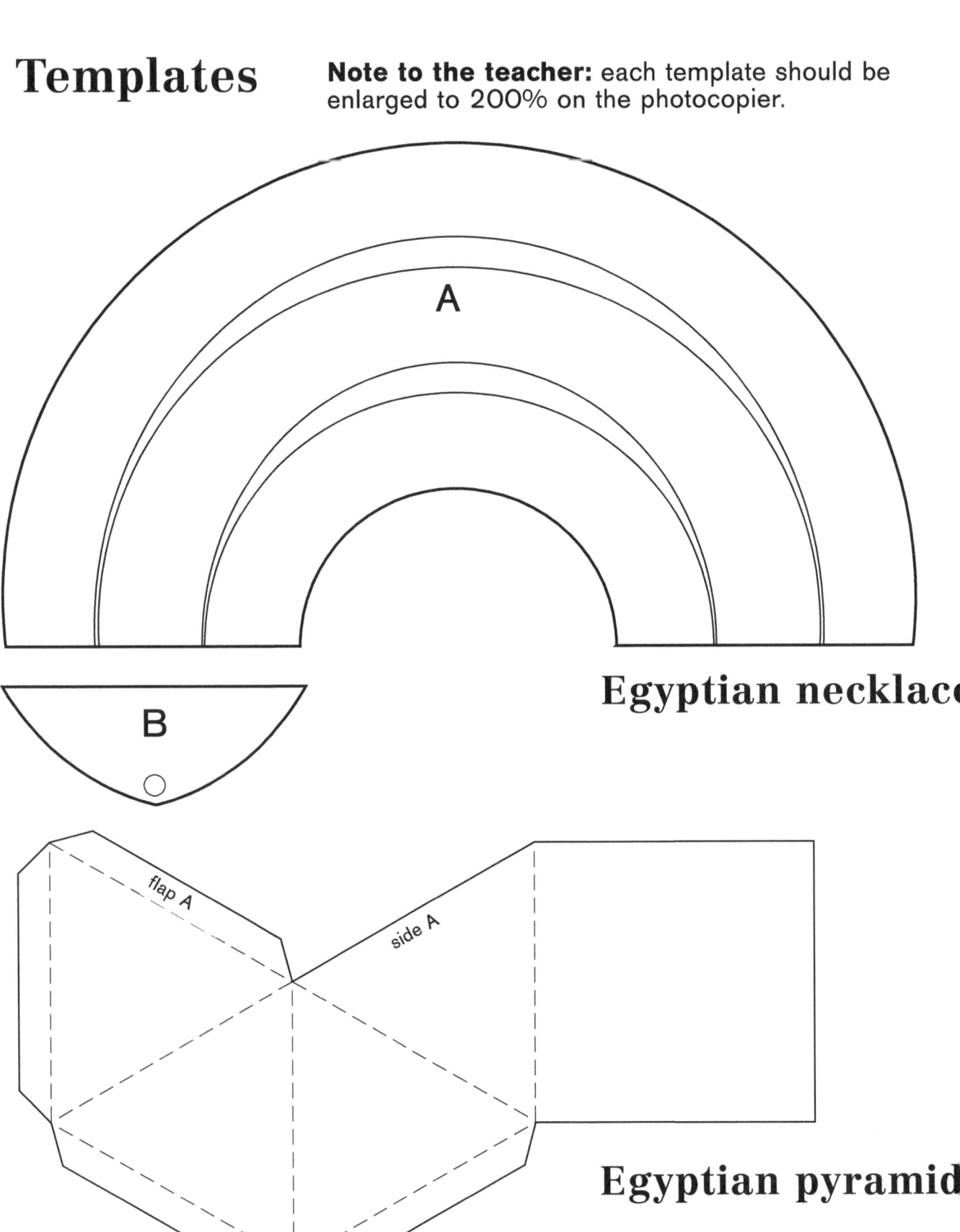

Egyptian necklace

Egyptian pyramid

Greek temple photo frame

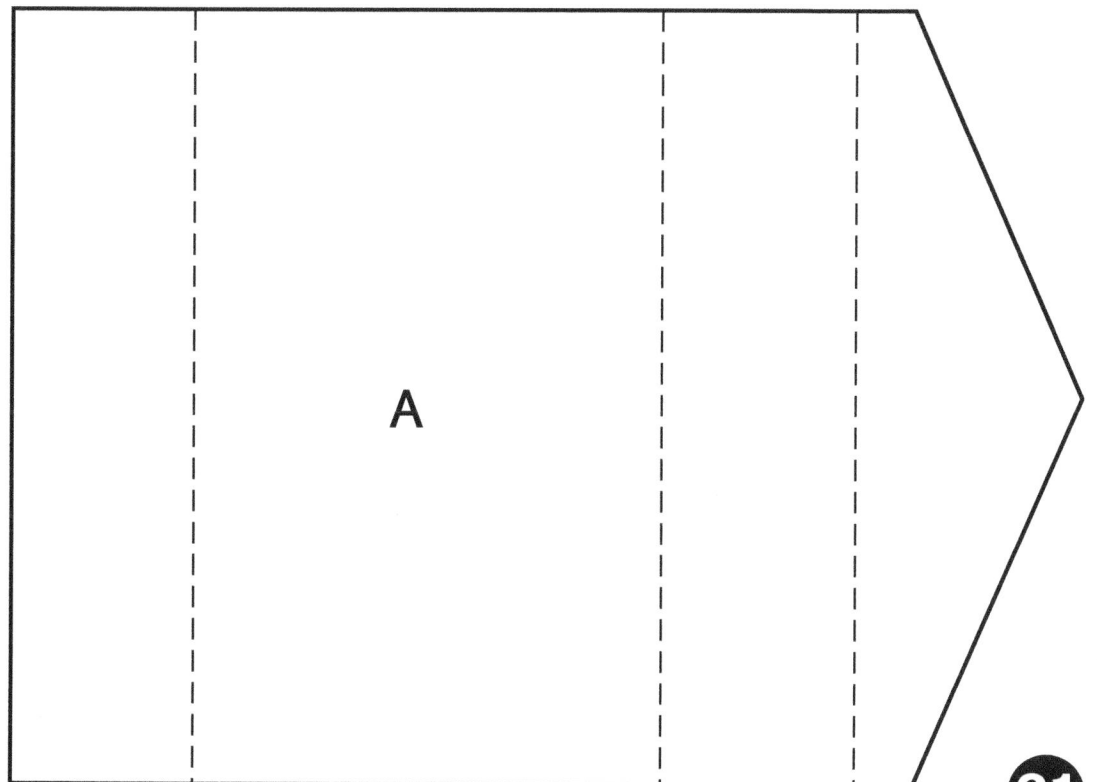

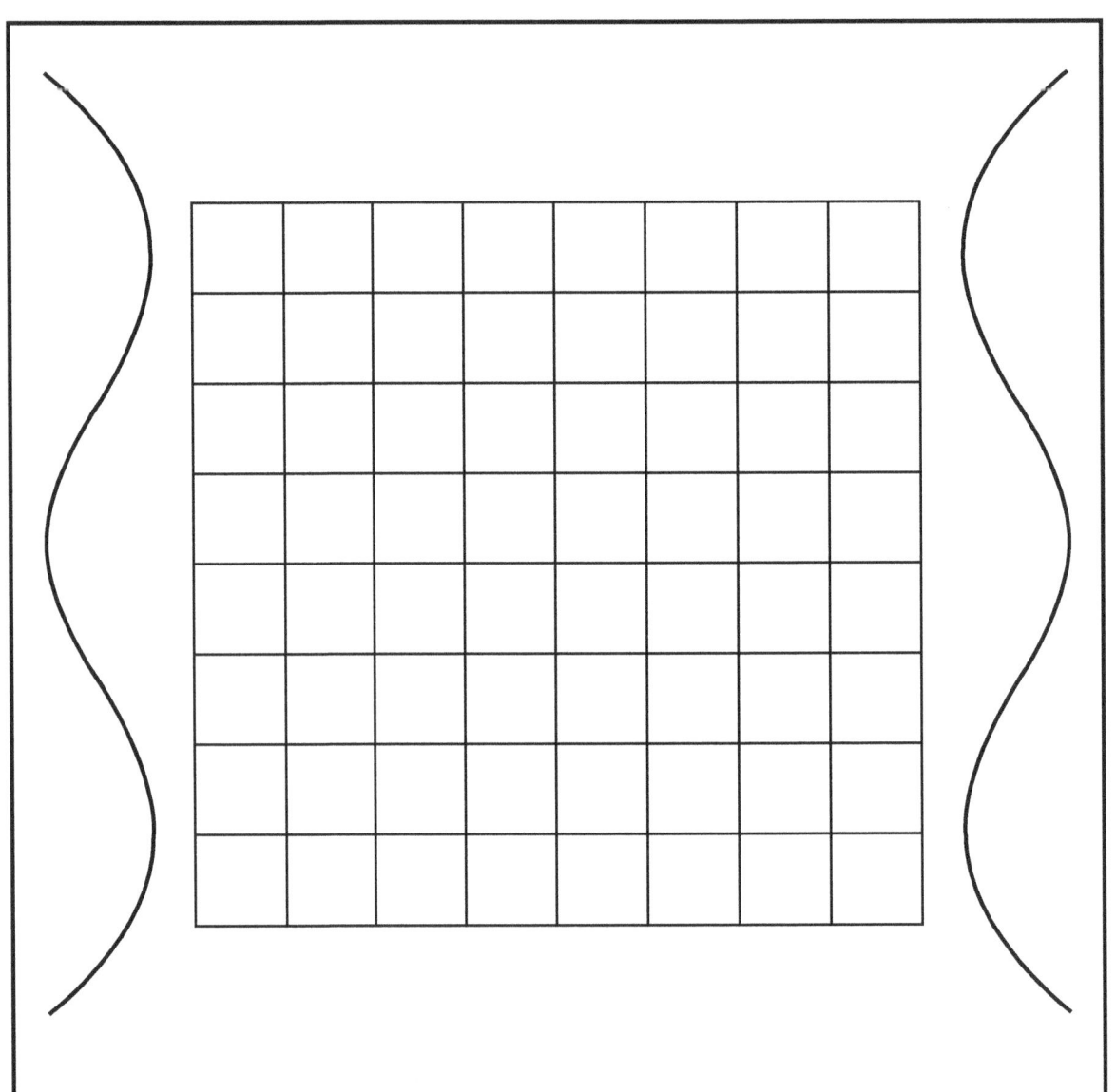

Roman draughts board

Bibliography

Title	Author	Publisher
Craft Topics: Romans	N. Baxter	Franklin Watts
Art from the Past: The Egyptians	Gillian Chapman	Heinemann
Crafts from the Past: The Greeks	Gillian Chapman	Heinemann
Crafts from the Past: The Romans	Gillian Chapman	Heinemann
The Ancient Greeks Activity Book	Jenny Chattington	British Museum Press
The Ancient Romans Activity Book	Ralph Jackson & Simon James	British Museum Press
The Ancient Egyptian Activity Book	Lise Manniche	British Museum Press
Craft Topics: Greeks	Ruth Thomson	Franklin Watts
Craft Topics: Egyptians	Rachael Wright	Franklin Watts

Index

artefact 4, 6, 7

coin 12

Egypt 6, 7

Egyptians 6, 7, 8, 10, 23

games 18

Giza 10

gods 12, 14

Greece 7

Greeks 7, 12, 14, 23

jewellery 6, 8

Mediterranean Sea 7

necklace 8, 20

Neptune 14

papyrus 16

Pegasus 12

River Nile 6

Romans 7, 16, 18, 23

Rome 7

scroll 16, 17

temple 14, 15, 21

Tutankhamen 8